FORTY YEARS OF SLAVERY: MY ENSLAVEMENT

By Tim Damianidis

This eBook was published in 2020 by

M. Damianidis

Copyright © 2020 Tim Damianidis

All rights reserved.

No part of this book may be reproduced, stored in a retrieval system, or transmitted in any form or by any means, electronic, mechanical, photocopying, recording, or otherwise, without express written permission of the publisher.

DIGITAL eBook: ISBN-13: 978-0646830469

PAPERBACK: ISBN-13: 978-0645522112

DEDICATION

In the name of Christ

WARNING and DISCLAIMER

CONTAINS GRAPHIC IMAGES

CONTAINS ABORIGINAL ANCESTOR PICTURES

CONTAINS COARSE LANGUAGE

By proceeding you accept and acknowledge any risks imposed by reading or viewing this book.

Contents

DEDICATION iii

WARNING and DISCLAIMER iv

WHERE DO I EVEN START? 1

THE ENSLAVEMENT 4

    The Oligarchy 5

    The Generation Gap 13

    Business and Migration 17

    The Ship Company 20

    The Police 21

    The Hospital 21

    The Club 21

    Education 24

THINKING OUT ALOUD 29

THE CONCLUSION 37

    A Fair Go 37

No Nursing State........................ 38

De-Industrialise........................ 39

Domestic Production and Manufacture..... 40

Racism and Discrimination............... 40

Jobs Allocation......................... 41

REFERENCES 42

BIBLIOGRAPHY 44

ABOUT THE AUTHOR 45

WHERE DO I EVEN START?

Where do I even start? The last thing I want, is to keep you in the dark. Do I start from the moment I was born or do I start from where my resumé begins? I could start from the days they forced us to wear pants instead of fustanellas or the days they pillaged the free cities. They are, after all, one and the same, not in person, nationality or race, but in psyche. This is about my enslavement for over forty years to a ruling class, I call the Oligarchy, that dominated and trashed my life. But now that they are doing the same thing to my children, I have to come forward in some way. Alone I can't stop them, but with you and others there may still be a chance. Who knows, among us there may still be an Achilleas or Perseus. But until someone stands up, things will remain the same. Who knows how many more like Christ will be crucified before things change?

I'll begin in 1969, the year I was born, in Cyprus. The British were forced to abandon their colonisation attempts because there was resistance in Cyprus. They were trying to colonise the island and turn a Greek-speaking island into an English-speaking one. The British came to the island to stave off the Russians from attacking Turkey in the Russo-Turkish wars. They came, they settled in and became comfortable with their new possession. The island had become a strategic centre for the British (Edwards, 2017; Stern, 1975).

The Cypriots, the majority of the island of Cyprus, wanted unity with the mainland of Greece. They called it the Enosis movement, and the head of the movement was assassinated, Archbishop Makarios (H. W. Brands, 1987). Meanwhile, the Americans came up with a deal with the British and Turkey, all the while, maintaining the agenda of keeping the Russians out of Turkey. The Americans would use NATO to build bases in the north of Cyprus, which was invaded in 1974 by Turks wearing "made in USA" boots, figuratively speaking. The British continued to hold their naval bases in the south of the island. By 1976 the island was split in two and the north was forcibly filled with Turks while the south depopulated due to mass migration away from the island. By 2020 there was still a vast majority of Greeks living on the island, still dreaming of unity with Greece. The puppet masters were those working for the British in the South and the American-Turkish alliance in the North. In between were families and people whose lives were disrupted. At that point, many lost everything they and their family-owned.

As for us? We left the mess behind us in 1972. We were told what was going to happen, so we left. Don't think we were weak. My father saw the tail end of WWII and a civil war which came to a conclusion around 1954. You have no idea what that means, dead bodies in gutters and on the side of the streets. Limbs and pieces of humans were being eaten by animals. Having water-soaked bread for breakfast on a good day when there was dried bread. Working for someone was not an option, everyone was working for themselves and very few paid jobs existed. The generation previous to my father's saw WWI and WWII and the Christian Genocide in Turkey. We come ancestrally from a place called Sebasteia in Anatolia, the place where the forty martyred themselves for what they believed. It was one of the places affected by the great exchange of populations where many Greeks left Anatolia.

So, in 1972 we arrived in Australia and became Australian citizens. By 1976 we were living in Perth, Western Australia. My father came over as a musician on contract to work and was sponsored to stay by relatives. My memories of West Perth as a young child were great. I had a beautiful upbringing among the kids in that locality, most were new immigrants. But by the time my parents were ready to buy a home, the urban sprawl had reached some twenty-minute drive from the city centre. We then lived, for a while, in Balga, a suburb north of Perth. The rich ethnics found refuge in the suburb Dianella. Others ended up in the slums like Balga, Koondoola and Girrawheen. Well, it took a decade or so before we moved to the less impoverished coastal zone. In reality, my father and his father probably had a better story to tell than I did. I will leave that perhaps for another time. But in any case, the journey till this point was hard and rough.

So, when did enslavement begin you may ask? Well, these things led to us migrating to Australia and to live ultimately for a long time among the poorest people in the country. Our migration was like going from one prison into another. The only difference was that there was food and much later on, a small surplus of money in Australia. Who controlled our lives in Cyprus and Greece? Who controls our lives in Australia? It most certainly isn't us or you, is it? Properties, assets, and money all meant nothing to us. In a flash, it can disappear, as it did many times over.

So where do I start? I will mainly focus on giving a historic view of the enslavement, a current synopsis of the enslavement that the world is suffering, finally, I will describe the average life of people through raising children, looking for work, running a business and analyse these aspects to formulate a better way of doing things in Australia.

THE ENSLAVEMENT

The enslavement began thousands of years ago, I was born into a modern-day version of slavery (Allen, 2005). If enough people are successful, it gives the false impression you can be too. So, they use that like a carrot to a mule to entice us to work. Now, I use the term successful the same way people use the term in everyday life, to have wealth and prosperity. But in reality, I know deep down that the only success is for those that have the balls to shake the shackles bear their cross and follow the Christ. Do I want modern success? Not much more than anyone else. I just wanted to put a roof over my family's heads and to provide a plate of food for them. It was my natural role as father to do that. But I was denied the most fundamental thing of being alive.

What we initially planned was to maintain our Greek education, build up a small amount of wealth and return back to Greece or Cyprus. So, we learned Greek, so that if we had to make that transition, we could do so effortlessly. The problems we faced were the forced English that stopped Greek from being taught and the removal of it from Academia. It was the same crap they did with the Aboriginals, after a few generations you had Aboriginals with British names and speaking English instead of their own language.

The British thought they were good at Colonisation but ultimately, they were only successful in a few places. Now I don't have anything against the Anglos-Saxons or British. Some blame it on the consequences and outcomes of the Saxon Invasion, or the War of the Roses, or maybe it was the Battle of Hastings and the Norman Invasion. Herodotus called these ancestral invaders and raiders Anthropophagoi (Herodotus, 2004). From what I gather, historically the term meant they devoured other people's lands, homes and resources through forcing them into near extinction. Look at North America compared to South America. In North America all the Indian tribes were driven to near extinction and forced to reside on remote lands. In South America, that came in contact with the Hellenistic people, they assimilated into large cities that still exist today.

In Australia they tried to do what they did in the USA, extinguish any possible chance of a re-emergence of the Aboriginal identity. I am not supporting the Aboriginal cause but I know what happened to them. The reason I say I am not supporting them is not because I don't love them, but because I would not be able to live with myself if anything were to happen to more of them as a result of my words. So, I won't mention in detail the stolen generation, the culling and genocides they enforced on those people. As one person said to me, we should be thankful they haven't struck our heads against rocks like they used to do to the Aboriginals.

The Oligarchy

Getting back to the enslavement issue and how it is structured let me show you an article I wrote on social media that describes it well enough: "Firstly, let me describe the scenario that fits all the countries in the world at the moment. They are operated and run by an Oligarchy. This Oligarchy has no common religion, customs, ethics or language. It is an Oligarchy of people with power and influence. Some presidents, prime ministers, and heads of state may have high positions but lack overall power and influence. So, their position does not automatically elevate them into the Oligarchy. This Oligarchy is dynamic and fluctuating, it is organic and large in numbers and small in numbers it has unity but most of the time not. You could say there are several Oligarchies working with and against each other but are ultimately one force or power and influence. For example, one power group may want access to oil in a country controlled by another oligarchy. The only way they will have access to it is through shares or war. Shares in companies are the way the elite work together and allow each of them to invest in mutual projects. When they are not compatible, they conflict with each other and compete with separate businesses and if that fails there is the risk of war.

Also, things like global organisations can be manipulated to serve the purpose of the few. This is why so many appealed against the establishment of world organisations. These become toy things for the Oligarchy.

Under the Oligarchy are the governments of the world, divided again into lower-level Oligarchies that have a few hundred and at most a thousand people governing millions (Winters & Page, 2009). These lower-level Oligarchies are the brute force that controls large populations.

Figure 1. Wyndham prison, WA, 1902 (Domain Public, 2023).

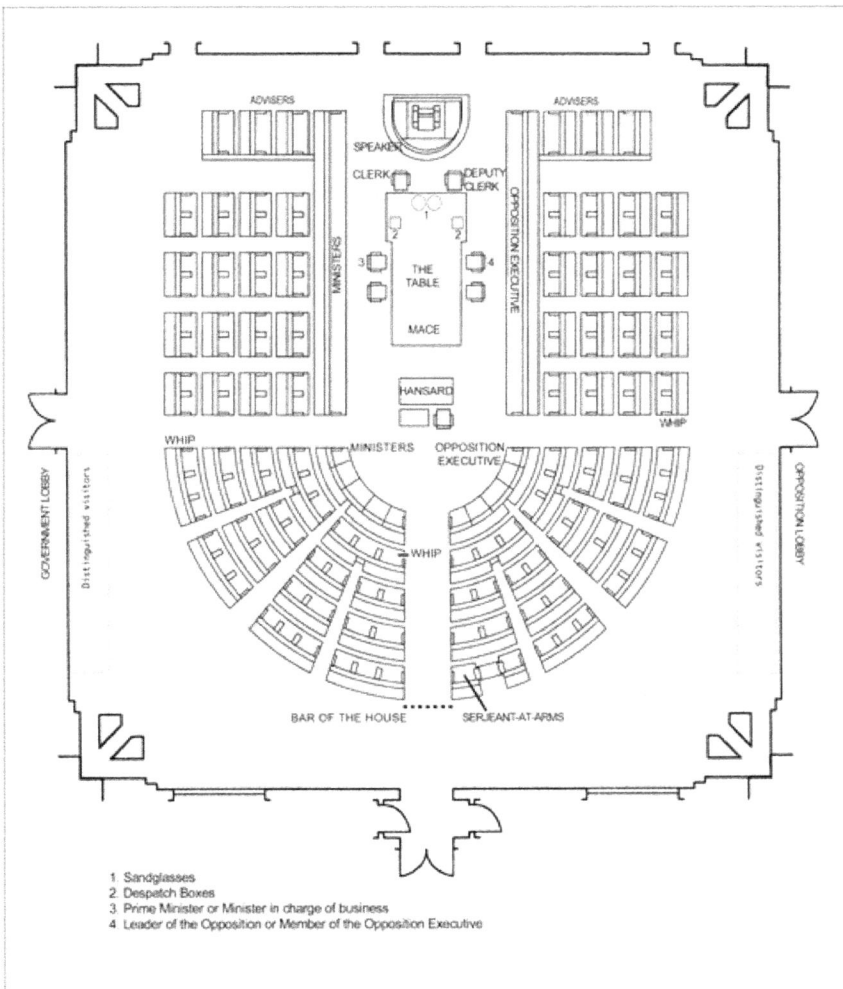

Figure 2. House of Representatives 2020, Western Australia (updated Australian Government, 2023)

They do it by every means possible, financial, material and through tyranny. There is no place that escapes these three factors, you may at times feel like quietly thinking this is freedom. It is an illusion built on the back of an army, police and a legal system aimed at controlling everyone for sake of the Oligarchy. You only need to read some of our laws and laws from other countries to realise they do not protect the weak. They are there for the purpose of regulating and maintaining the way that the Oligarchy interacts with humanity. For example, the Oligarchy that controls the United Nations, the World Health Organisation and many more global entities also control every profession and establishment that sources these organisations as authorities and sources of the truth. Without some hesitation to turn away the atheist reader, it is worth pointing out that the only true Authority and deliverer of Truth to the Christian is Christ. I will not say more, other than we have replaced God with men acting as Gods within a circle of friendship we know as the Oligarchy. What I say here is true around the world, there is not one place exempt from this control.

Some of you may wonder who makes up such an informal organisation and the reality is that it is everywhere present through the power and influence some people have. I am not going to mention their names but there are many involved and come from the church, masonic establishments, elite clubs and organisations, temples and mosque figures and so many more from all places including the military of some countries. They are powerful, friends and co-workers for the most part. They are not just the rich because power is more than having wealth. As an example, a candidate for a particular government in Asia sent his resumé and his agenda through social media to a very powerful person involved with the computer and other industries. The position the person was aiming to get was president for the country. This shows how power is perceived in some people and others are attracted to it in hope of self-benefit.

So, in this world of Oligarchies there is no such thing as Democracy. There is only the elite leading the many. Even the establishment of government is not immune to the workings of the Oligarchy. They infiltrate and use every device to leverage more and more power. When some people speak out, they are criticised, mocked and if that doesn't work they are muted in many numbers of ways.

There are many people suffering what Christ suffered, not all at once and in the exact same way, but parts of his suffering are lived through everyday people. A Democracy with Christian ethics was a vision many held dear to them for thousands of years. But now even the word Democracy has been played and toyed with so that Oligarchies are given equal status.

You see, when the few lead, they are easy to steer and direct and manipulate, when it is the many that lead, as is the case of a Democracy, they can't control the people. So, these governments we see on our planet are not the pinnacle of authority, power and influence, they are a tool for those that control them.

Are they invisible? For the most part you do not see their actions visibly but the year 2020 is a fine example of how a viral outbreak was handled more or less exactly the same by every lower-level Oligarchy (Government) under their (The Oligarchy's) control. They did this because they control the World Health Organisation (WHO). The WHO issued recommendations that obliged every lower-level Oligarchy and member state to follow. Why? There is speculation that they want to make money from vaccines. But there is more brewing politically in terms of a potential world war. This is all based on fleeting evidences found on the internet in terms of social media and other sources. The ability to substantiate it and prove it is lacking therefore yes, they are invisible. Some refer to this dynamic as the "invisible hand" (Basu, 2011; Varner, 2011).

We can't prove anything of their hidden agendas and their behind-the-scenes workings. So, we typically carry onward without much attention to the real problems we face. As we turn a blind eye, we in turn give rise to more of the same to occur. The conspiracy theorists don't have all the answers they just know something isn't quite right with the system we have. I am here to explain what the problem is.

The Oligarchy controls everything down to the social problems we face in our lives. You may think it is impossible to ban and rid our society of drugs. After-all, all the communities in the world share similar problems. But the reality is that the so-called drug problem is a derivative of certain freedoms that are in place to corrupt everyone. For example, when we install public transport, the ramifications are that juveniles have a way to go wherever they want. Including to visit drug dealers, carry drugs and essentially gain the freedom to travel vast distances away from their homes.

The laws that were changed to accommodate non-nuclear families, resulting from divorces, stated that children could decide where they slept. So, you could effectively have your child sleeping in a neighbour's house without the legal power to remove them, if that is what the child wanted. When they get into a stranger's car, they are allowed by law to do so and the stranger can take them anywhere the child wants to go. So, you see the so-called political progress has intentionally stolen people's children away from them. No different to the way the "lost generation" worked in Australia and the way Turks made Janissaries of Greeks. It is done using subtle legal methods. Now of course people will argue these things, because this is where things vary around the world. But there is always a side effect for every action we take and it is important that we start seeing these side effects rather than masking and hiding them. The Oligarchy doesn't want our unity and co-operation, it is chaos and argument that they thrive on.

What is our purpose in life? Is it to be married? Some of us won't. Is it to have children? Some of us won't. Is it to accumulate wealth? Some of us won't. The underlying purpose of life is twofold. It is to govern yourself and to do so with love and compassion for all humanity. To govern yourself within the restraints of the Oligarchy is a difficult process. To do so under a Democracy is harder to initiate but easier to do once established. So then as Christ already said, look at the log in your eye before you remove the spec in your brother's eye. Meaning, let's start with our own faults and problems before we look at those of others. The things that stop us from seeing the good and truth need to be removed from our lives (Byzantine Majority Text NT, 2023).

I am a professional who is concerned with the Safety and Health of workers. But in almost every organisation the purpose of the role is to ensure the organisation does not get penalised or suffer a loss of any kind as opposed to seeking of a better work environment for the worker. The police are the same, they join with pure hearts but end up serving a different master through the corrupted laws the Oligarchy has sculpted. The same is said of politicians who thought they could change their nations and society and bring about wonderful things, only to realise they too have masters and people of greater powers and influence.

One more time I will speak of the Oligarchy. Now in context with the fact that they are visible in some respects as a class from Aristotle's societal divisions. You see Aristotle divided society in five groups, Farmers, Military, Merchants, Tradesmen and Professionals. These categories still apply today. What we have allowed to occur is the Merchant class to corrupt all the other classes and by doing so controls all of them. In India it was said to us in our schooling that Farmers once controlled the other five groups. In other places it is the Military or Soldiers that dominate. In ancient Egypt the professional class of Clergy and Doctors dominated society. But overall, the problem the world has today is that the Merchant class has been given much too many freedoms and as a result they have corrupted the other classes and the society that upholds them. The Oligarchy that I mention is from all these five classes but the Merchant class is the one with the most money to motivate change and for whatever reasons has grown over the globe as the largest of these five classes.

I believe that Christianity was the faith tied to a Democratic system whereby the Meek and devout will inherit the earth. Christianity is not tied by political means but the faith emerged at a time when Imperialism sprawled over once city states, and Christ spoke against it in a subtle way. That is to say, he gave messages that asked us to obey our oppressors give to them what belongs to them but always believe in the truth. So, if a Democracy with Christian Ethics was ever to emerge it would do so with great difficulty as the governments would first need to tame the influence of business and the merchant classes. I say governments because they are the last bastions of the invested interest people have. There is not much that can be done unless we somehow reverse so-called progress by dismantling the way the Merchant Oligarchy works. Our governments are one of the ways that can help reverse things but who will educate our politicians and give them guidance to do so? One way is to eliminate competitor banks and disallow private banks, eliminate corporations and their share system and so forth. But in turn would this create the same old problems of war and extreme poverty? These are things that deserve to be studied properly before attempting to bring balance to the system and it's five classes. There is a solution, Pericles gave a basic income to all citizens for participating in government. Each City owned its own resources and there was a balance in the classes. He offered Not a dole nor a social security payment but an income that made every citizen a politician and leader. I say it is a matter of study, but some of us already have solutions. It is a part of Democracy that everyone forms their own solution and ideas. "

This is how I feel because this is what I have seen in my life, the puppets have masters and it is they that have, through their device and system, strangulated my glory and that glory we all deserved to have. They killed me and everyone else on the planet at birth, so we have nothing to lose. These people filter who gets a qualification and who doesn't, they determine who has work and what kind of work. They determine who has a home and who doesn't. Also, don't think for a moment racism and discrimination aren't strong and well. The number of times that I was told just before a job interview, "you are here for the equal opportunity act", were many. As if to say they were satisfying the law by inviting an ethnic to an interview. You see the Oligarchy doesn't always directly deal with us because millions are serving their agenda. Even I, myself, was involved with enforcing their laws to some degree.

The Generation Gap

From a young age, children are taken away from their parents through a soft mechanism that is called compulsory schooling. They train them to be soldiers by giving them a basic understanding of things and lots of sporting activities to maintain their health, agility and warrior readiness. They changed the laws as I described earlier to reduce the authority of parents over their own children. This in-turn gave children a lot more freedoms than they ordinarily would have. So, outside the realm of compulsory schooling, children are not influenced by their parents as much as they used to. A few generations ago, fathers and sons would almost always be doing the same job. Further back and surnames were given based upon what your family did for a living. Now they gave children choices that were artificial and, in a way, forced on them. By this I mean that some choices aren't ours to make or possible to make without external intervention. Yet they make it seem as if we have that option. Like choosing who they travel with or where they sleep.

This is a sign of slavery where by the system fosters our children. The only thing the government doesn't get involved with is providing meals and a room to sleep. They save money that way. The parents outlay all the living expenses and the government provides everything needed to "educate" and steer the child away from the parents. Where necessary, money is even given by government as welfare to aid in caring for the children. From the age they can hold a gun, sixteen, they are given rations in the form of welfare payments of their own. This describes most of the Australian children, the ones born here and raised here.

It should be evident then that the children are taken from parents softly. They get educated and trained, they are then given freedoms and choices they normally wouldn't have, then they are given money to supposedly liberate them. If you can't see it, let me give you an example. The child learns to be away from their parents and family by going to school. They then train and educate them on the things they want them to know. They give them physical exercise and training to maintain their battle readiness through subjects like sports. Then they give them choices to go see drug dealers through subjects like Health. They even provide public transport to allow them to get to the drug dealer's house. Then they setup payments that kids can use to buy drugs.

Meanwhile the airwaves and streaming media are showing open signs of debauchery and profanity in both visual and lyrical forms. These put illusions into the heads of children and they teach them to dance and sing differently to their parents. Indeed, the generation gap, is an illusion forced on children and families with intent.

How many on welfare are doing drugs and alcohol? The stats come from a number of different sources and each one varies too much to consider one or the other more accurate. There is a small increase in the number of unemployed people doing drugs and alcohol but not so much as to say that the problem is exclusive to being unemployed. It simply means that the small percentage that use illicit drugs in society may be employed or unemployed. The difference being on how they got hooked. No-one has documented if the first illicit buy was by using welfare payments. So again, by observation and survey of youth, I have discovered many have their first buy on welfare, they also continue to use it and are prone to selling it to supplement their welfare income and habits.

This is the underlying environment that everyone seems to overlook and if I am to talk about enslavement then hooking kids on drugs is the next level of slavery. Not only are they slaves to the system but once addicted they become slaves to those that control their drugs. I was fortunate and escaped without being hooked on drugs. I was however, exposed to so many people that were drug dependant that it made my direction in life clearer by examples around me. I was very interested in being a musician and spent a lot of my time playing guitar in my youth. There was a circle of groupies and lots of drugs and alcohol at our jams and parties. I was there for the music alone and took a bird's eye view of all the debauchery that existed at that level. They were unemployed on welfare and addicted. I was working, into music and not addicted. I was fortunate to not have become wrapped up in that scene also.

Figure 3. Hungry Jacks Bans Service to Teens (Achenza, 2023)

Business and Migration

Work gives us some freedoms that are positive and reinforcing. That is to say that whether you are employed or not you are a slave to the system, but having money gives some freedom. The system is designed so that you have a myriad of choices, but none to be free. Free to self-determine and rule over your own affairs, instead you have others doing that for you. So long as that is the case, we will never know what freedom truly feels like. Money, as I mentioned, does give some freedom in this current system. It gives us the ability to pay for almost anything we want. But not all things can be bought and that is where a system that praises money fails.

Now I want to talk about business. So, you might wonder for a moment why there are so many Ethnics running shops, farms and small businesses. In most cases, these ventures are just scraping through. The reality is that they are essentially all the people no-one wants to hire. Who do they want to hire? Well, some may jump to the conclusion that it is purely the Anglo-Saxons with some salt and pepper thrown in for legal purposes. However, the work force is mainly a mixture of ethnicities and Greek and Aboriginal are one of those that are given fewer chances. The moment my resume hits the desk of a "non-ethnic" recruiter the first thing they do is throw it in a pile of names they can't pronounce. But of course, there are other people recruiting and the ethnics are just as bad. This is why we see Chinese shops, Greek shops, Italian shops and so forth. If they aren't doing the same old tribal thing and selecting their own, then they are recruiting across the board and what stands out is that to appease their masters, like the ones giving them contracts, they fill positions with the appropriate race.

Now in my field of Occupational Health and Safety they hire from a small pool that is like a family. It uses family members in a variety of operations, so they end up recycling the same people over and over again. The inlet for new people is so narrow only a small trickle is allowed in and through. The British and ex British still dominate senior Safety and director positions. Now this is not very well known in most other states in Australia because of some peculiarities that I will describe. For now, it is worth mentioning that the state I live in, WA, has the largest mining sector and most of the British investments import Brits and ex Brits into these operations. In other states which focus on other industries like hospitality, the servants are mainly ethnics.

Each Australian state has a slightly different multicultural experience. The destination for incoming ethnics is different for each city in Australia, they crammed the Middle Easterners in NSW and VIC, Chinese in VIC and they crammed the British into Perth. The others were distributed around the country. Most of the Greeks arrived in Victoria and some earlier arrivals, that came on Italian passports, arrived in Perth.

Perth therefore evolved and had a lot of the Northern suburbs filled with ex Brits and Italians. The Southern suburbs were mainly Australians from several generations but mainly ex British citizens with a marked presence of Italians. The Italians also filled Perth and there was like a Germanic alliance formed by the groups that were settled into the region. I say Germanic because the Germans wanted to ally the British and Italians so that is what was found in large population numbers in Perth, Germanic people, British and Italians. The many that came on Italian passports were, however, ethnically Greeks and they created a small enclave. My generation was a small influx of Greeks allowed to settle in Perth during the mid 70's. They were different to those Greeks that landed on Italian and other passports.

So many Australians complain that the Chinese have taken over, guess where those complaints originate from? Victoria, where they were taken during their immigration. Some complain that the British are arriving in droves, guess where that may be? Perth! Then there are those complaining about the blacks or the Greeks or any such minority depending on how many arrived as immigrants. In any case the immigration isn't the problem it is the fact that the country is unable to employ equally everyone in proportionate numbers. It doesn't have the capacity to hire both males and females let alone immigrants. So, to maintain a growth rate the British companies employ British citizens and ex British citizens, the Government agencies are heavily Anglo Saxon, but they have become more proportionately representative of the population in the last decade. Not every department, but some.

Now the previous was based on observance and some may argue that the census shows different statistics. The 2011 Census shows 13,500 Greeks in Perth. But this is a play of words. There are 13,500 people born in Greece living in Perth. The number of Greek decent or ancestry if we add up all the free-range Greeks of Calabria, Sicily and Neapolis etc, plus all the Greeks of Egypt, Anatolia and India that made their way to Perth plus their children and grandchildren and great grandchildren. Well, you get the picture, there are hundreds of thousands of Greek descent people living in Perth.

Now of course, after being born here you earn the special title of Australian. But if you still carry a non-Anglicised name you are discriminated against when looking for work. This is why the Aboriginals have all those Anglo-Saxon names, but even that didn't prove enough to mask identity. So now almost every agency and company ask two discriminatory questions to make sure none of these Aborigines actually end up with a job. The two discriminatory questions are 1. Are you Aboriginal descent or Torres Strait Islander? The second question is 2. Do you have a disability? If so when and how did you get it and did you claim compensation etc So you see there are some things going on that are peculiarly the norm.

So, there you have it, the big multicultural slum that filters out all the people they consider family from the people like myself that don't deserve a chance. Am I dreaming this? Hardly. This is the brutal reality of the world I live in. Some people find it easy to gain employment and others don't, but what if I told you that I had submitted 1000's of resumes over a period of three years and none resulted in a long-term job. I gained a few contracts here and there but never a solid job of the type you need to buy a house and put food on the table. I struggled my entire life to find a decent job. I wanted to enslave myself further and sacrifice my life to give my children a better chance than I had. I wanted them to be empowered and able to break the shackles. I tried everything I tried going back to university when the children were younger, I finished a college diploma I started and operated numerous businesses all with about the same support as those hiring. Eventually I managed to secure a Graduate Diploma in OHS and start up another company called Thoulia.

Now I will walk you through my enslavement as a volunteer. You see some of you get renumerated for the work you do. I on the other hand was used and disposed of from a young age onwards. I didn't let any of this affect me spiritually but it certainly did affect my life and that of my family's.

The Ship Company

While I was studying for a TAFE/College Diploma I entered voluntarily to work for a ship builder in Western Australia. I worked there for almost a year. I even went to the extent of working as an advisor for the existing Health and Safety manager and later when he went on holiday, I was given the management role. But when it came to paid work, they didn't offer any. Instead, when they found out I was going to Cyprus as a Safety consultant in the shipping industry, which I did briefly, they asked me to come back and tell them what I had learned.

The Police
Again, I volunteered years later. I did work that I can't confess to. I wasn't a snitch but you could say I did some police work without being a paid police officer. They couldn't write a letter of reference or anything. They instead fed me a hamburger at a restaurant and told me thank you for your service.

The Hospital
I am not sure what to make of this place, I even wrote songs against them for their excessive import of British citizens into Australian jobs. You see it is a long story: One day, a newly arrived Brit sat next to me at a lunch induction table and said "I saw an advertised position in the UK and it guaranteed a job and help to relocate. I didn't think I would get it but I did."

I told him "Indeed you are lucky the university across the road graduates 400 nurses every year and almost none of them get employed by the Hospital."

So, I was making noises and they got rid of me one way or another.

The Club
I trained for and worked as the Approved Manager for the club and did not receive a single cent for my efforts. I had to resign because It was such a dysfunctional environment that I couldn't continue working in such an environment. It was volunteer mayhem. But in the process, I was in charge of paid staff while I remained unpaid. This was the model they developed. This was another situation in my life where for whatever reason people would rather exploit me than help me.

Now I mentioned a few places out of my resume where I worked and was not renumerated properly for the work and effort, I put in. Or where I volunteered and wasn't given any help when I asked for it. Even though some were truly voluntary positions, the expectation to reciprocate even with a letter of reference didn't happen. All this had a serious impact on me and my family. There is a lot I didn't say and lots of examples I wouldn't raise, like working for the church, community groups, helping animal shelters etc.

Because of these experiences, and more, I finally tried my hand at self-employment. I did dabble in business in my youth as well but that is another story. All the businesses I started failed to fulfil their role, but none became bankrupt, to date. They were successful in operation but unsuccessful in achieving a high income. The same thing stopping me from securing long term high paid work is the same thing that stops me from getting anywhere with a micro business.

You see the Australian psyche is a little confused. They rush in to buy from large corporations but they don't bother helping small business. In fact, people go out of their way to avoid dealing with small business. That and also the small businesses are more expensive than their large competitors. Even your friends get jealous that you might make more money than them and yet they can't see that 80% of businesses fail within 2 years of start-up. So, help is thinly applied. For a business to survive it needs to have enormous capital and money backing the venture. But more importantly it needs support which I didn't have.

So, what do I say? I was trapped with a qualification, experience and knowledge and yet remained unemployed for long stretches. Yet I saw others go so far ahead in their pathway to success. Was it me? My qualification? What exactly was it that prevented people from hiring me? What was it that stopped people from buying from me when I started my businesses? I should say I had several regular and supportive customers, and they weren't related. They spent their money on worthwhile products and we had a good business relationship. Needless to say, they were all ethnics.

So, it wasn't the typical things like advertising, we did that well, customer service, we did that well that too. It was the fact that our marketing and financial limitations let us down. Large companies could spend significantly more amounts but less of a percentage of their earnings. So, where I would spend thirty to forty percent of our revenue on advertising and marketing, big companies spent a thousand-fold more but only one to five percent of their total revenue. Add to this that I had to reach a lot more people before getting anyone to respond than a big company like Coca Cola. Almost everyone still knows their name and product decades after starting up. My businesses on the other hand were advertised to many but lacked some kind of response. It was like falling on deaf ears.

I knew all this before starting a small business, I even knew that the business wouldn't survive more than a year or two, but they did last for decades, just scraping through. The statistics were against us. But I did it anyway because we had no other choice. In one business, that I operated, it ended with us selling someone's products and they made the money while we gradually spiralled down. Our profit margin to stay competitive reached as low as 10% profit on some items. As you can guess, it was too small a margin to maintain the huge effort needed to keep the business alive. I tried lots of different types of businesses, each one I couldn't see how to lift it off the ground with what I had.

So, in the end I had a break down, a significant mental health problem. I got to the stage where I lost my colour vision for a significant period of time, I was temporarily colour blind. The amount of depression that I had was heavy and I had some personal losses, the people I looked up to the most began to pass away. For a decade I was almost entirely crippled but still running around trying to earn a living to support my family.

Education

I took a look at what I had done in my life and realised that the only way I could get ahead from where I was standing was to get another qualification. Now at one University there were a few people who despised me for whatever reason. They would duck their heads into my classes just to say "We will never let you pass". Now you may think it odd that some lecturers would act this way. It was because I refuted back in the 90's some of the idiocy that was introduced into science by Western universities. I sat there and argued with lecturers in-front of class members some specific things that were in my eyes not science but propaganda. I can't remember the exact specifics; I was brighter back then. But the argument was something like:

"So, you think that atoms are made of smaller particles and that for convenience's sake we should name them and they include electrons and protons and neutrons. You then say that these things constitute the smallest divisible object, we call an atom. Now for a moment consider what the Greek philosophers already said. The atom by literal definition means "the singular self" that is it has no constituents. On that point modern science teaches the atom is divisible and the philosophers say it is not. Then, when we ask, are the smallest components of the atom divisible, the German investigation in the early 90's stated that the proton and neutron and electron are divisible. So that smaller elements than the ones we named exist. Now I ask you when you finally reach natures' limit, that is the point of where things are considered to exist or not to exist, what then of the smallest possible thing that can exist? They couldn't answer me. So, I then proceeded to say that what if, what you call an atom is not The Atom but some material that is divisible and in common existence? What if I say to you that when you stop dividing the material or object and cannot divide it any further you will find the atom. You see the atom is the smallest a piece of material that is allowed to exist before nature does not allow it to exist. It is a limit on how small things can be. Just like the tallest mountains have a limit to how high they can reach or how big a planet or celestial object can be before it breaks up. But don't let me give you hope in finding it, because to see it you will need to reflect light or energy like light such as electrons or smaller such energised material to see the atom. How then can you reflect something smaller than the limit to which nature allows? So then, the atom has yet to be discovered, it will never be seen and is indivisible, as the philosophers once spoke."

So I was unable to get a degree or higher education, I felt prevented in a soft way of course. I felt immense anxiety two decades later trying to achieve the same thing I had set my mind on in my youth. But I had to do it. Nothing would change my life if I didn't change something about it. So, I marched on again down the road of enslavement. I had no other choice really.

Where could I go? The Aboriginal communities in the outback were being strangulated from all resources, how could I join them. Should I join the Hutt River Province? They ended up being sued and taken down by the government. Should I march into the outback with my family? They just wouldn't follow at the age they were at. Trust me I did try, I even put a personal ad asking "does anyone want to start a new city" by migrating and living as a tribe. I didn't get any responses. So, what was I meant to do? I even tried to get rid of my car and the trap of buying tyres, brakes and fuel on a regular basis for the luxury of sitting on a motorised missile. The local council sent back a letter saying they wouldn't allow me to buy a horse, to drive my intended chariot, because the land I was on was too small for the city by-laws. Yes indeed, I can't hunt and I can't fish anymore without money and licenses and so forth. I can't simply side step the system because every path away from it is blocked by laws against it.

Seriously, what could I do in this scenario? I thought go back and do a degree or a qualification that will get you a better job. I had experience, knowledge and some qualifications in Safety. When operating businesses for myself or others I drifted always to an interest in Safety. So now I was searching for a real job and I wanted to compete for a real income. To match that ambition, I needed a decent qualification. But it was more than that. I had kids I wanted to go to university and not make the same mistakes I made. I wanted to pave the way and show them that it was possible to get a qualification and a higher education. Also, it was something personal that I wanted to achieve. So, as I was looking around, I realised Edith Cowan University had suitable Graduate positions. This time I kept my mouth shut until after I graduated. And yes, there was a scientific component to which I simply shut my mouth about. I graduated in 2018 with a Graduate Certificate and in 2019 I received a Graduate Diploma. Thousands of job applications later and I was still an unemployed slave. So I had to write something and say something.

If anything is to change then at least these words may inspire someone to modify or change the way they do things. I am not calling for a full-scale revolution to declare a direct democratic state, although I'm not against the idea either. In fact, of all the qualifications I have, starting a new country and running it democratically is one I had prepared for since my earliest Greek schooling. But what I am asking for is that we stop going down the same path that we are on. Now by "we" I'm including myself as an Australian.

I am not a Greek or a Cypriot citizen anymore, I spent almost all my life in this country, Australia. I may have been born elsewhere but several months later I was an Australian citizen. All my children were born and raised here too. When I went back to Greece they called me a Xeno ("foreigner") and behind everyone's view I am treated like a stranger in Australia. I don't belong anywhere except where I put my foot down and call it home. That place is Australia.

So, again, I have done everything I can, alone, to make my life better, to enslave myself further and sacrifice my life for my children, but again, I am an unpaid slave. I live a meaningless existence in a world I have no control over. Realistically, I scoff at the elections here or elsewhere, the masters of puppets don't get elected it is the puppets themselves that get elected. So where do I stand? I have played along with their joke of a system for a lifetime and still I have no reward for pretending everything is ok.

In between jobs, I forgot to mention, I played guitar and tried to sing and earn an income. I play the guitar well, but my singing needs too much work to make it viable. I wrote many songs, of which twelve were destined for an album. But my application for a grant was rejected because I didn't organise things well enough. For example, I was hoping to audition musicians, but they wanted the musicians to be ready to go. Anyway, I have written politically friendly songs that replace my burning desire to say political stuff. So, I have been doing things and keeping active. I am working without being paid at the moment. I have been this way on and off for a very long time, most of my life was spent struggling like this. This describes my position now, so with or without work I am tied down without the ability to do the things I really want to do. I have thousands of useless choices served to me on a platter and I don't have the choice of being free. What have I said that wasn't already said before by our philosophers?

Now, there were good times. I worked and ran and operated businesses for others and myself. I did ok with those businesses but nothing stands out as a major success. Sure, there were successful moments and even times we thought life was good and we were happy and content. But the overbearing reality was that to raise a family a person needs a house and money in this system. They need so much materials, in fact, that they become not only slaves to the system, but slaves to other masters who control the jobs and money.

I didn't mention a myriad of things like the wage slave argument or the debt slave argument or the technology slave argument and so forth because I wanted to express and highlight our God given right to shelter our families and put food on our tables. I wanted to write about the day-to-day problems people face as parents and as people searching for employment. I wanted to express that no matter where we sit in the hierarchy of our economic and social status, we are all slaves. Appending a prefix to it like work slave, debt slave, technology slave, wage slave etc doesn't change the fact that the systems around the world have squashed us into servants, employed and unemployed.

THINKING OUT ALOUD

As a child I learned Greek in a pigeon cage. That Greek set me free to an extent. Why? I could read, with some difficulty, the original Bible, the works of the philosophers and a myriad of knowledge that empowered me to be one thing, a leader of myself. That is, it gave me the tools and the knowledge to be a leader of my own destiny. Wherever I relied on someone else, I was denied help. It's like raising your hand while you are sinking and people stepping on you to duck you deeper constantly. But the Greek language opened my eyes to a world founded on Christian and Democratic ways. Funny, isn't it? Very symbolic of where i live. The pigeons and Greek language represent freedom, and the cage the system that we live in. Now I am not saying everyone should go learn Greek, but at-least people like me should put that knowledge into the system and allow others to have their eyes opened to the empowerment that self-reliance and self-leadership can have when guided by geniuses that lived thousands of years ago.

Aussie battler was a term used literally once, but you can see my battle, right? People like me are too many to count, call us whatever you want, the composition of Aussies that suffer this story are varied and many. I am not alone or unique in this experience, it describes hundreds of thousands of people, perhaps millions. Even those ex-Brits suffer as do the Greeks and Aboriginals and so forth. What can I say to you that would make things better, not only for me but you too?

What can we learn from this story so that my children, your children and everyone in the system can have what Australians consider a Fair Go? Well, the underlying thing is that no-one gives. By this I mean "no-one gives a shit", a typical Aussie saying. In fact, apathy is so wide spread that people would rather pull up a chair and watch an accident unfold than to go out of their way to help. How can you make people care? You can't. You can entice them, give them choice but you can't make anyone do anything that they don't want to. An old Aesop fable describes an old man and a young child walking together on a large rock. They come across to a crevice and the young man jumps over the crevice. The old man still nimble and capable of stepping over the crevice decides to halt. The young boy mentioned the crevice was very shallow, very narrow, it wouldn't even fit the old man's leg in it if he were to step on it. But the old man refused because he was a coward. The moral being, you can't give courage to a coward. In the same way when a person is apathetic, they lack the ability to understand a situation from another perspective. They maybe apathetic because they haven't gone through the same things themselves. They maybe apathetic because they were raised or genetically at a disadvantage to care. I remember many people walking around my teen life claiming they were "too cool to care" about serious issues like religion or politics. Of course, a small percentage will listen to reason and even a coward will find courage at times. So too the apathetic will sometimes feel their emotions too.

This apathy leads to a huge number of our problems. You see most of the instinctive actions we take centre on non-emotional, mechanical actions. That is to say that as humans we tend to like a little bit of routine in our life. But that routine can have a huge impact. For example, the routine in the way we hire, fire, train, teach, discipline and so forth; routine in the way we buy, sell, support and evade products and services. Apathy, results in sayings like "We should be thankful." Or "We are blessed." Or "We are lucky." But isn't that being good and caring you may think? Caring is using our surplus, be it material or otherwise, to pass it onto others. Excesses in any and every positive form can be passed on through our actions. Actions, after all, speak louder than words. It is biblical that we take action and show our actions above all else. So love can be achieved by not having that special pile of job applications that see the bin before the others. Love and caring can be giving a person a chance based on their experiences and qualifications instead of who they know in the organisation. Love through caring, instead of being apathetic, is necessary before all else.

The next matter is that the last thing we need is a system that cares for us. Because ultimately what is done in the name of caring for us is frightening. The only care we need is to be free to direct ourselves. I was taught that by some great teachers and I would not let them be silenced now.

Now that everything is lost, my life of enslavement is coming to it's twilight years. Now that everything has come full circle and my children are undergoing the same bullshit as I once did. Here I am still pretending that everything is ok, advising the kids "no matter what your teachers say you have to believe it." I know they are feeding children lies in almost every subject. Even the dances they dance, and the music they listen to are all lies and make believe. But the kids believe it and it makes up their reality. Sad but true.

This is how they care for us, and we have to pretend we are going along with it. But what for? Do I want to live in a shit hole that they created in every country around the world? Well, no, none of us do. So, we have seen how they "care" for us. Do we want more of this type of caring? No, we don't. But do we want sincere reflection of morals and ethics to apply to everything we do? Yes, although typically apathetic, the people that do generally care want a system that is genuine and a reflection of their morals and ethics. It is so vivid in my life at least; this way of thinking formed the reason I chose Safety and Health.

I didn't want to work for a company that put people's lives at risk. But I ended up being what I spoke of. The guy that covered up shit and pretended it didn't stink so that the companies I worked for would be able to continue their day-to-day business of killing people for sake of making money. Now I didn't exactly cover up anything legally but I sure wasn't there working the job I was supposed to be doing i.e. keeping workers safe no matter what!

There were a few mining companies that wanted to change the scene Hugh Morgan was one of the guys I met that had a team that was willing to commit to the safety in respect of responsibility and authority. But management at the time and in almost all companies was against the law ushered in by the harmonised Work Health and Safety Acts in Australia and worldwide.

These laws made directors responsible and punishable for safety and increased the fines while the whole problem was an energy-based problem. The bigger the fire you play with the higher the number of people burnt. It was, with all due respect to my university and all those in the field, a farse to believe that punishing the tall poppies would somehow make the shorter ones grow.

There is little benefit to these laws but the fines were modernised which I guess was necessary. But the real problem was the energy issue. For example, the mode of operation the design and engineering, the magnitude of the potential energy and way of doing things in general are the factors that affect the occurrence of the energy, the way the energy is used and its interface with humans, and finally how the energy is extinguished and its impact on closing down. I know I have lost many of you with these generic words, I'm trying to write a philosophy, and I am reluctant using specific examples. However, to get this point across I will give a specific example: The mining companies have huge trucks bigger than any other industry. These trucks are involved in the death of workers over time and across the mining industry. The energy is stored in the big assed truck. The interface is the small, comparative, human thinking he controls that massive energy with a number of pedals and a steering wheel. The reality is the opposite. The energy owns the operator. It always will unless it is reduced and that is our problem. Do we go back to shovelling ore in wheel barrows where the energy is smaller and the worst that could happen was a busted back, or do we keep doing things big for sake of big amounts of money.

There are definitely some things that will take time to fix, but we need to know what the problem is. De-energising the industry and breaking down some of the industrial revolutionary "advances" to more human level processes are going to take generations to dismantle and create respectively. Will this create more jobs? Yes, it will. Will it reduce the extent of the injuries? Yes, it will. Will it solve the OHS issue? No, it won't solve the problem but the lower the potential energy the better it is for workers.

So, what else can we say to make things better? Local and domestic production for the local market. You see when we gauge income in Australia with other places, we have a cap of around $180,000 before there is the maximum amount of tax taken out, so there aren't any people earning such amounts of money that they can start their own operation. Not only that, but big franchises from the USA come to Australia and one of the problems they face instantly is there is actually a very small market. We are like a wasteland without any surplus cash and our rich are average people earning incomes of around $180,000 a year.

The truly rich and wealthy obviously found loopholes to accumulate vast amounts of wealth and income that come under the radar as company earnings. But even that way they earn significantly less than equivalent or comparable businesses in the USA. Look at McDonalds Australia with McDonalds USA. You don't need their stats to appreciate which earns significantly more money do you? I'm not going to quote the stats, just search for them on the internet. I'm not a sympathiser for these types of corporations and don't have anything to do with them actually. But their advertising is so effective that almost every Aussie knows their name. I wonder, at this point, if my brand names will ever catch on. I even wonder if anyone will buy a bar of soap at the price, I have set it. Indeed, I plugged my own business in, who else will do it for me?

To me the market is near dead. To others it is going well. But overall, the profitability of the local market is less lucrative than foreign markets. What I mean is that, if you have a business in Australia, the demand is lower and the pay is lower and the profit is lower than anywhere else in the developed West. This is not true for everything but certainly most private ventures can't survive in the Australian business climate.

For a long time, we have been importing technology and exporting resources. But never have we been given the chance with our current market to re-introduce all those clothes factories, car manufacturing and all the other businesses that once thrived in pre-dollar Australia. Australia was alarmingly self-sufficient and could have taken the path to becoming a major exporter of technology, products and services. Instead, bad leadership, the Oligarchy and external forces forced Australia to sell its blood in the form of resources like sheep, wool, minerals, iron and other similar things.

Without the substantial local jobs around, without manufacture and production, Australia gets put into a situation where the job market is restricted. Some argued that Australian jobs would go from blue collar to white collar and that roles would shift, but that didn't happen. In fact, the opposite happened. When we compare the working person in the 1960's to 1970's, one basic income was capable of buying a house over twenty years, along with sizeable amounts of savings or investments. People still struggled back then also, there were people left on the fringes but the huge majority were catered for. You could liken it to well looked after slaves.

Then, since the early 1980's onwards, Australia has suffered several blows to its economy. Always taking a fore interest to the foreign pressures put on it. Recently, China slowed down it's trading with Australia in response to US and Australian military defence contracts. So as you can see the foreign powers, or the Oligarchy, influence greatly the fact that Australia hasn't stood on its own two feet for many decades.

I am almost done. We can't instantly stop racism and discrimination, even the laws against this behaviour are a joke. You would think that by this time and age it would have stopped, but age-old rivalries carry on the same old way. People just can't get a grip on the simple rule "Love they neighbour".

I could have joined the police force when I had the chance, maybe even joined the army. I even said to some corporate proposition for work, "I refuse to be employed in a position where I pretend to be looking after the safety and health of the employees." So I had choices or chances to "go with the flow" but for my personal reasons I decided on my own identity. I didn't want to become like everyone else, I wanted what I was and who I became, to be called Australian. I say this because if I was to assimilate completely, I would have changed my name, dyed my hair a lighter colour, anglicised my name and renamed all my children's names. Then I would have worked for companies that were seemingly with the Oligarchy. Pretended to be on their side and done what all the ass lickers ended up doing for hundreds of years in this country. I would have never learned about the philosophers or the faith. So here I am stating the obvious. Stop the racism, discrimination and hatred. For a Democracy to work, and no we don't have one, you need to "Love thy neighbour." The first and most important rule. By doing this alone, you can instantly see, that we treat everyone fairly and give them that "fair go."

The final matter, not because I couldn't go on and on, is the way jobs are allocated. They are not transparent. When you get told, "we wanted someone who multi tasks" you are being told we want a woman or female. When you are being told we want someone "who has emotional control" they want a male or man. This cryptic way of writing and a few other statements in job descriptions seems fine. It gives us a heads up that the job role is gender specific. But when it becomes racial? Are you Aboriginal or Torres Strait Islander? Or when it becomes personal Do you have a disability? "Have you ever claimed Compo? "Have you ever been convicted?" Does it still seem fine? And when the people are selected are they put in piles of names you can pronounce and names you can't? When the manager has a short list have, they added the ethnic forsake of mention. Like the token black guy in a movie. What exactly is happening in the decision-making process? What exactly are the criteria that are being looked at during interviews? What is being said to applicants when they are rejected and seeking advice? I lost several job opportunities because I didn't fit the gender, age, background and so forth. How do we make the job selection process honest? The same way we make government honest: Democratic lots. If you have the qualification and experience then your resume goes into a shortlist which can be actually large, based on the number of applicants. Then all the candidates are invited to draw lots in person so they can witness the drawing of lots. The person drawing a lot is the candidate and if they get the required lot, they obtain the position. "They drew lots to see who would take his garments"(translated from Byzantine Majority Text NT, 2023).

THE CONCLUSION

I will be brief with my conclusion. The six points described in the analysis are that:

1.) we need a fair go,
2.) we don't need state nursing,
3.) we should de-industrialise but increase manpower safely,
4.) increase domestic production and manufacture,
5.) eliminate racism and discrimination from society,
6.) and there should be a better system of how jobs are allocated.

A Fair Go

In all honesty this country needs to start caring. If people are going to succeed in this country, they need a platform that allows it. The apathy that drove previous generations has to be curbed into one that cares for small business and commercial undertakings. There can't be this extreme left view that all businesses are capitalistic ventures. Small business are family operated attempts to put a roof over their heads and food on their plates. They shouldn't be seen as attempts to somehow capitalise on profits. They are far from that type of operation.

Corporations mask their investors through shares, anyone from anywhere in the world could be investing in a corporation. Then there is the fact that large businesses have a tendency to have no loyalty because their shareholders come from everywhere in the world. So, they invest in foreign markets and use foreign labour and factories. They exploit people at every turn to make profit for the sake of making profit and have little concern about what the business does, it's product and services.

In a quest to be cheap they have flooded markets with products and services that are highly competitive but not necessarily high in quality. It's like comparing mum's burgers with takeaway burgers, one is made with quality ingredients and prepared in a high-quality manner while the other is using the most cost-effective ingredients and is tossed together typically by a fifteen year old. So, what I am trying to say is that we should care about small business and small manufacturers and industry. There should be an instant support from people for such things. Because in doing so we are creating a domestic market, one that we and our children will need. It is giving all Australians a Fair Go.

No Nursing State

The Last thing we want is Australia to become a nursing state. To give us caring and trying to manipulate things for our so-called benefit. But at the same time some consideration should be given in educating children that most small businesses are run by mums and dads or people who are local and trying to get ahead.

Some things that were made available to children in terms of freedoms and allowances in some ways lead the underprivileged to assume that working is a second option. There should be merit for those that want to work at a young age but I believe that there is a much higher dropout rate for kids that find work before finishing school.

I would say that children that think they know what profession they want to work in, should be given opportunities in industry to sample the work and environment through practical programs. Parents or friends with businesses could guide children by showing them the ropes. Of course, what I am suggesting is that practical work experience in real paying jobs should come as a priority for teenagers. This reduces their idle time and promotes a work ethic in them.

Having said all that, I still think school is for those seeking the truth, for academic purposes. I would think that streams be made for those seeking to go to university or to become professionals should be given some form of work experience in their chosen fields, if it is possible of course. But for this to happen requires government to give incentives to businesses to hire mid-teens, even if it is to make coffees, use a computer or file documents. From there, internships could be achieved and more as the students matured. Overall, the empowerment to succeed should be shown and not held away from children. The nursing state mentality needs to somehow rewind and pause from all the things it has done in the name for caring for us.

De-Industrialise

Buying smaller trucks, or smaller machines, reducing the energy humans are exposed to by following key principles such as eliminate certain types of industrial work, substitute risks, engineer better and safer interfaces by asking safety professionals or somas to input during design and engineering phases, provide safer lower potential energy procedures and finally protect them with PPE that actually works. There is no point in wearing a hard hat and boots in a truck that can't stop due to brake failure.

It is a bit of an oxymoron for an Industrialised country to consider de-industrialisation. By this I don't mean stop production. I mean do it in a more humanly accessible way. Reduce the potential energy stored in the materials and processes used by humans. It is one thing to be asking from an ivory tower for more ore to fill trucks, while on the shop floor the truck brakes and drive shafts are failing, due to over filling. So we need to be in touch with what is physically possible, what can be done to minimise harmful energy and take actions to deal with it.

Domestic Production and Manufacture

It is recommended that for Australia to get ahead it needs to change some of the things it does. This can be achieved in a number of ways. The most fundamental problem we face is rolling out enough jobs to hire everyone. At the moment husbands and wives are competing for jobs. Meanwhile, all the local hubs for manufacturing are diminishing considerably and our domestic market is not viable. You see people are used to buying cheap mass-produced products and think that they are entitled to such cheap products. The toilet paper hoarding incident during the CoViD19 crisis was a stark reminder how local manufacturing is vastly important to maintain and support. Instantly after this, locally made soap and hand sanitizers were stocked and sold by a huge number of operations. This indicates to us that under a protected environment Australian product can compete. Also, the psyche of Australians needs education and understanding about how important it is not to buy the cheapest but the product that gives back into the community. Small business supports mums and dads trying to earn a dollar.

Just like how we go out and get a trade or qualification, the country has to prepare a professional body that is competent. Why aren't we making technology of our own? If it wasn't for all the small companies like mine, Australia wouldn't be manufacturing anything significant. So, preparing a professional body capable of contributing to domestic manufacturing is paramount.

Racism and Discrimination

Needless to say, it's alive and well in every facet of this world. If only we could find a way to send it on its way. Like a vine choking the true vine of its breathe in life. So too, racism and discrimination serve to kill us too. It doesn't benefit anyone except this circle some people call cronies and others call the Oligarchy and friends. It ruins lives and stops people who actually are good at what they do from having a chance at all. Now having said that, I think we should be a little more cautious of who attends graduation services at universities. I stood at the back of some engineering students that booed the national anthem when it was sung. I felt like stripping them of their graduation clothes and qualifications. I think this shouldn't be a restriction imposed but one of nationality. You call yourself an Australian citizen then you sing the national anthem. If you are not then you shouldn't be at a service with other Australians.

Jobs Allocation
A more democratic system of advertising, finding and applying for jobs should be in place. I spoke of drawing lots and maybe that is the best way possible to ensure that jobs are catered for everyone. Ultimately, it doesn't matter who you hire provided they have qualifications and basic experiences needed for the job.

With love in Christ, I send you my small message in hope that things will get better. If not in my life time maybe in yours or the next.

REFERENCES

Achenza, M. (2023, 2023-02-01). 'Will not be served': Strict ban on diner group. *The Australian*. https://www.news.com.au/lifestyle/food/eat/hungry-jacks-franchise-bans-eshays-from-ordering-at-perth-store/news-story/2873948ca18a7dfc1c2f9fd688e26005

Allen, B. (2005). Alexander the Great: Or the Terrible? *The Hudson Review, 58*(220-230). https://doi.org/10.2307/30044758

Australian Government. (2023). *House of Representatives Seating Plan – Parliament of Australia*. https://www.aph.gov.au/About_Parliament/House_of_Representatives/House_of_Representatives_Seating_Plan

Basu, K. (2011). The Theory of the Invisible Hand. In *Beyond the Invisible Hand: Groundwork for a New Economics*. Princeton University Press. https://doi.org/10.2307/j.ctt7rv3c

Byzantine Majority Text NT. (2023). Byzantine Majority Text NT. In. Constantinople: Patriarchate of Constantinople.

Domain Public. (2023). australian-aborigines-chains-1902.webp. In australian-aborigines-chains.webp (Ed.). https://rarehistoricalphotos.com/.

Edwards, A. (2017). Defending the realm? https://doi.org/10.2307/j.ctt21216mg

H. W. Brands, J. (1987). America Enters the Cyprus Tangle, 1964. *Middle Eastern Studies, 23*(3), 348-362. https://doi.org/10.2307/4283189

Herodotus. (2004). The Histories (G. C. McCaulay, Donald Lateiner, Trans.). In: Barnes & Noble Classics.

Stern, L. (1975). Bitter Lessons: How We Failed in Cyprus. *Foreign Policy*(19), 34. https://doi.org/10.2307/1147991

Varner, C. (2011). Reviewed Work(s): Beyond the Invisible Hand: Groundwork for a New Economics by Kaushik Basu. *Monthly Labor Review*, 53.

https://www.jstor.org/stable/10.2307/monthlylaborrev.2011.11.053

Winters, J. A., & Page, B. I. (2009). Oligarchy in the United States? *Perspectives on Politics*, *7*(4), 731-751. https://doi.org/10.2307/40407076

BIBLIOGRAPHY

A.A. Vasiliev - History of the Byzantine empire
Adam Smith - The Wealth of Nations
Aristotle - The Complete Surviving Works
Herodotus - The Complete Surviving Works
Homer - Iliad & Odyssey
Karl Marx - The Communist Manifesto
Livius - The Complete Surviving Works
Michael Psellus – Chronographia
Plato - The Complete Surviving Works
Plutarch - The Complete Surviving Works
Sophocles – incl. Antigone
The New Testament
The Septuagint
Thucydides – incl. Peloponnese Wars
Treadgold, Warren - The Revival of Byzantine Learning and the Revival of the Byzantine State
 - A History of the Byzantine State and Society
University of Cambridge -The Cambridge History of the Byzantine Empire c.500-1492
William Shakespeare – Selected Works

ABOUT THE AUTHOR

Tim Damianidis is a business person and family man with connections around the world. He has a Graduate Diploma in Occupational Health and Safety and has worked in numerous businesses.

www.ingramcontent.com/pod-product-compliance
Lightning Source LLC
Chambersburg PA
CBHW060222050426
42446CB00013B/3144